Sit Sit

Written by Sarah Rice

Illustrated by Anna Kazimi

Collins

sit

sit

3

tap

tap

5

a tin

tip tip

a pan

pat pat

tap tap

sip sip

11

tap tap

sit sit

14

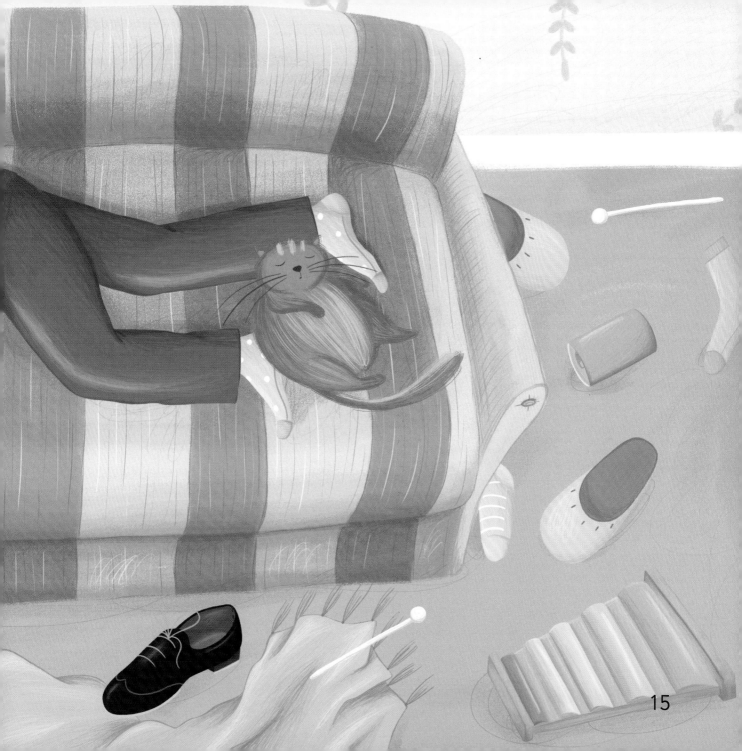

 Review: After reading

Use your assessment from hearing the children read to choose any GPCs, words or tricky words that need additional practice.

Read 1: Decoding

- Say the word **sip** on page 11. Ask the children if they can sound out each of the letter sounds in the word **sip** and then blend them. (*s/i/p – **sip***)
- Now ask them to do the same with the following words:
  tap   sit   pan
- Look at the "I spy sounds" pages (14–15) together. How many words can the children point out that contain the /s/ sound? (e.g. *sleeping, scarf, shoe, sandwich, sock, sandal*)

Read 2: Prosody

- Model reading each page with expression to the children. After you have read each page, ask the children to have a go at reading with expression.

Read 3: Comprehension

- For every question ask the children how they know the answer. Ask:
  - Can you remember some of the things the boy in the story did? (e.g. *made music, danced, sat down*)
  - Do you think the girl was enjoying the music and dancing? Why?
  - What happened at the end of the story? (*the girl clapped and the lady nearly spilled her drink*)
  - What do you think happened next?